W9-BYH-867

Fall

Kay Barnham

PowerKiDS press™
New York

Published in 2011 by The Rosen Publishing Group Inc.
29 East 21st Street, New York, NY 10010

Copyright © 2011 Wayland/
The Rosen Publishing Group, Inc.

First Edition

Senior Editor: Claire Shanahan
Designer: Ruth Cowan
Picture Researcher: Louise Edgeworth
Concept Designer: Paul Cherrill

Library of Congress Cataloging-in-Publication Data

Barnham, Kay.
  Fall / by Kay Barnham. — 1st ed.
      p. cm. — (Seasons)
  Includes index.
  ISBN 978-1-61532-567-2 (library binding)
  ISBN 978-1-61532-571-9 (paperback)
  ISBN 978-1-61532-572-6 (6-pack)
  1. Autumn—Juvenile literature. I. Title.
  QB637.7.B37 2011
  508.2—dc22
                                                    2009045848

Photographs:
Alamy: Dan O'Flynn Title page, Inga Spence Imprint
page, Andre Jenny p4-5, Enigma p7, Steve Atkins p10,
Dan O'Flynn p13, Grant Rooney p16, Inga Spence
p17, Louise Batalla Duran p19; Corbis: Claude
Woodruff COVER, p15; Getty Images: Schultheiss
Selection GmbH & CoKG p9, p14, Mel Yates/Stone
p18; Istockphoto: p6, Ina Peters p11, Nickolay
Bolshackov p12.

Manufactured in China
CPSIA Compliance Information: Batch #WAS0102PK: For Further Information
contact Rosen Publishing, New York, New York at 1-800-237-9932

Web Sites

Due to the changing nature of Internet
links, PowerKids Press has developed
an online list of Web sites related to
the subject of this book. This site is
updated regularly. Please use this link
to access this list:
http://www.powerkidslinks.com/sesn/fall

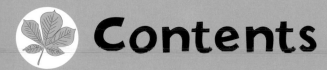

Contents

The Seasons

There are four seasons in the year. The seasons are called spring, summer, fall, and winter. Each season is different.

In the fall, the days grow shorter.
The weather becomes cooler.
The fall months are September,
October, and November.

Fall Weather

In the fall, there are fewer dry, sunny days than in summer. Clouds hide the sun. Some days may be foggy.

There may even be frost at this time of year.

6

Blustery, cold, and wet weather is common. You will need to wear clothes that keep you warm and dry.

In the fall, there may be strong winds and heavy rain.

# Fall Trees

Leaves turn sunlight into energy. This helps trees grow. When the weather is colder and cloudier in the fall, the leaves are not needed anymore. They fall from the trees.

Leaves change color before they fall.

Trees also drop their seeds at this time of year. New trees will grow from these seeds in the spring.

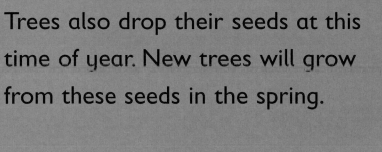

Horse chestnut trees have shiny seeds called horse chestnuts.

9

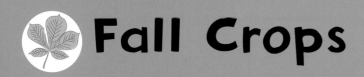

Fall Crops

Farmers plant seeds in the spring. They grow crops of barley, wheat, corn, and oats. By the fall, the crops are ready to be harvested.

The farmer is harvesting this field of wheat.

The grain from crops can be made into food for us to eat. Some of the grain is fed to farm animals.

Grain can be used to make bread.

Animals in the Fall

In the fall, cats, dogs, foxes, and squirrels grow thicker coats. They are getting ready for cold weather. Some birds fly to warmer countries.

This dog's thick coat will keep it warm during the colder months.

Squirrels spend the fall gathering nuts.
They hide the nuts in safe places, so
that they will have food to eat
in the winter.

Fall Fun

The nights get longer and the days get shorter in the fall. But there is still enough daylight to have fun outdoors. Windy fall weather is perfect for windsurfing and flying kites.

When it is windy, windsurfers can leap into the air!

Why not go on a nature walk?
You can collect crunchy leaves,
horse chesnuts, and acorns.

How many different
colored leaves
can you find?

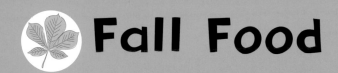

Fall Food

Lots of different fruits are ripe in the fall. Blackberries grow in hedges. Orchards are full of apples, pears, and plums.

These plums can be baked in a pie.

Look for ripe vegetables, too.
Mushrooms grow wild in fields.
Farmers and gardeners harvest
pumpkins, zucchini, and squashes.

Can you think of a use for this ripe pumpkin?

Fall Festivals

In the United States and Canada, fall happens toward the end of the year. Halloween takes place on October 31. People dress up as witches and ghosts.

Halloween is a very popular holiday.

Veterans Day in November
is when people remember those
who died in wars. Diwali is an Asian
Indian and Nepalese festival held
in October or November.

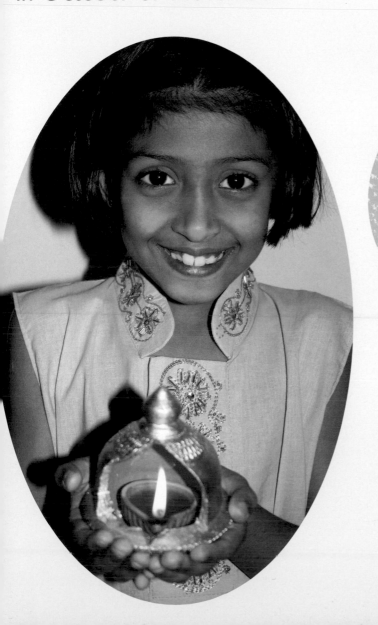

Diwali is
also known
as the Festival
of Light.

Why Do We Have Seasons?

We have seasons because Earth is tilted. As Earth moves around the Sun, different parts of the planet are nearer the Sun.

In the **spring**, our part of the planet moves toward the Sun. The weather grows warmer.

In the **summer**, our part of the planet is nearest the Sun, so the weather is hot.

In the **fall**, our part of the planet moves away from the Sun. The weather grows cooler.

In the **winter**, our part of the planet is farthest from the Sun. This means that the weather is cold.

It takes a year for the four seasons to happen. This is because it takes a year for Earth to move around the Sun.

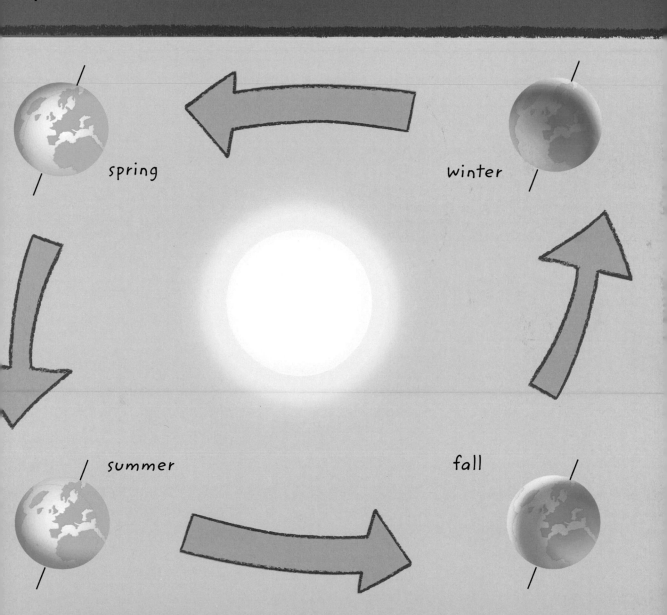

spring

winter

summer

fall

Make a Birdseed Feeder

Make a birdseed feeder to give the birds a healthy snack in the fall. You could leave out a shallow bowl of water for them, too.

You will ne
• a pine co
• string
• a bowl
• 3½ ounce (1
mixture of bir
sunflower se
grated cheese
raisins
• 3½ ounce (1
piece of la

1. Tie a piece of string around the middle of the pine cone. Make sure it's nice and tight.

2. Put the lard and mixture of dry ingredients into a bowl. Squeeze the mixture together with your fingers until you have a sticky mixture.

3. Carefully mold the mixture
around the pine cone.

4. Put the pine cone in the
refrigerator for an hour, so
that the mixture gets hard.

5. Hang the birdseed feeder
from a sturdy tree branch,
and watch the feathery
friends visit!

Glossary and Further Information

Asian Indian something that comes from the country called India

blustery when wind is gusty and fierce

crop plants such as barley, wheat, oats, and corn that are grown for food

foggy when the air is damp, misty, and difficult to see through

frosty when it is cold and icy

grain seed such as corn and wheat that is used for making food

harvested when crops are gathered

horse chesnut hard brown seed that grows on a horse chestnut tree

horse chestnut tree a big tree that has dark brown seeds

Nepalese something that comes from the country called Nepal

Books

Fall
by Nuria Roca
(Barrons Educational, 2004)

Fall
by Sian Smith
(Heinemann Library, 2009)

Watching the Seasons
by Edana Eckart
(Children's Press, 2004)

Index